THE BLOOD OF JESUS

Its power and how to benefit from it

A book by

DEREK AGGREY-SOLOMON

Dedication

This book is dedicated to the Lord Jesus Christ for shedding His precious blood to give us redemption.

Contents

Foreward

I am highly elated and honoured to be chosen amongst the lot to write a foreword to REV. DEREK AGGREY-SOLOMON`S book, THE BLOOD OF JESUS CHRIST.

I have always admired and loved Pastor Derek`s prayer life, his devotion to the things of the God and his burning desire to see the growth of THE KINGDOM OF GOD. He has been obedient to the voice and the promptings of the HOLY SPIRIT and is therefore not strange that he chose to write a book on THE BLOOD OF JESUS CHRIST which is appropriate and unprecedented at this perilous times, when most people including ardent Christians seem to have given up on themselves and are being mocked by friends and relatives ,with some even questioning, if there is still power in the BLOOD OF JESUS CHRIST, which was shed over 2000 years ago for our total redemption in this modern and technological world.

As a servant of God, I have personally witnessed the workings of the matchless Blood of our LORD and SAVIOUR JESUS CHRIST, and have seen uncountable people from various backgrounds receiving freedom, healing, fulfilment, salvation and deliverance from all kinds of calamities, misfortunes and many more.

THE BLOOD OF JESUS is very core in our REDEMPTION and SALVATION as Christians and therefore any book, write-up or discussion on this UNCOMPARABLE and UNCONDITIONAL SACRIFICE must be tackled with all the importance it requires, since without THE BLOOD, our salvation would have been incomplete and baseless.

The shedding of this precious Blood ,which cannot be valued or be compared to any other sacrifice ever made in the history of human existence was as a result of the pure and indescribable love our Father in Heaven has for His children. "For God so loved the world that HE gave HIS only begotten SON [JESUS CHRIST] that whosoever believes in HIM should not perish but have everlasting life ".

This text from the Bible summarizes the importance the Father Himself attaches to the shedding of THE BLOOD OF JESUS CHRIST as a means to redeeming every human being, because once you accept and believe in HIM [JESUS CHRIST] you automatically become a beneficiary of this great sacrifice of the Blood.

As Christians we have to remember always that the shedding of THE BLOOD OF JESUS CHRIST was the greatest gift ever, and therefore we should not downplay it`s significance, power and benefit to the course of our existence as depicted in this book.

The content of this book, which has been inspired by the HOLY SPIRIT is to give the Christian more insight into the complex issues relating to the shedding of this precious Blood for his or her redemption and salvation from the evils of this world, and also as a guide and a light on the path of the non-Christian who is yet to understand the intricacies of the power in the BLOOD OF JESUS.

In conclusion , it is my prayer that whoever finds this book [THE BLOOD OF JESUS CHRIST] to read shall not perish but shall have abundant life and repossess his or her possessions in life in the mighty name of JESUS CHRIST, since the BLOOD can and shall never lose its power over sin, diseases, curses, bondage, death, poverty etc

REV. BOB ASARE
FAITH ALIVE MIN. INT.
SEKONDI
GHANA

Preface

We do take a lot of things for granted as humans and especially as Christians. We find ourselves just going through the motions of religious activities without taking time to find out from the scriptures the reasons why those things are so.

Such is the case with the blood of Jesus. We find ourselves for example going through the motions of Jesus' cricifixion every Easter and for most of us, it is just like drama. We fail to find out why it had to happen and the benefits we do have from it as people who believe.

Many songs have also been sung about the blood of Jesus, many of which we sing just to tickle our emotions but once again, very few of us actually go behind the scenes to find out why the blood of Jesus keeps being mentioned.

In Hosea 4:6, we are told that we mostly perish because we do not know the things we are supposed to know. There is so much power in the blood of Jesus. It is actually the foundation of our faith. It is the ultimate atonement for all our sins. It is the only currency by which we can purchase our liberty from all the works of the devil. We can only access the presence and power of God by the blood but most of us suffer unnecessarily because we do not know.

Those who know a little about the blood also do not know how to make use of it. Until you know how to apply knowledge, it is only a burden. I pray that by this book, we will know more about the blood of Jesus, the power that comes through the blood and most importantly, how to appropriate such power for our benefit.

I am very confident that your life will change for the better. You will take back the power which the enemy has stolen from you over the years due to ignorance. You will rise up to heights you never imagined you could.
You will manifest your authority as a redeemed Christian and most importantly, you will become more militant in your christian life. You will love Jesus more and will let everyone know about Him.
By the time you finish this book, your Christian life and your prayer life will take a new turn that will amaze you and everyone around you. You will now

sing with understanding, the song of the redeemed.

May God bless you as you read. May the Holy Ghost open your eyes to the divine truth. May you behold wondrous things that will change your destiny for good. May the eyes of your understanding be enlightened so you can comprehend and apprehend all that is rightfully yours in Christ Jesus.

The time has come for the sons of God to manifest their true sonship and yours starts here. You are blessed to be a blessing.
Remain lifted in Jesus' precious name.

Acknowledgments

My first appreciation goes to God Almighty for His Holy Spirit which continues to give me divine insights in His word, making me a blessing to my generation.

Secondly I thank God for giving me great teachers of the word who have opened my eyes to amazing revelations in the word over the years. I thank God for the lives of Bishop David Oyedepo of Winners Chapel Worldwide, Rev. Kenneth E Hagin of Blessed Memory (Rhema), Derek Prince, Pastor Benny Hinn and Bishop Dag Heward Mills for teaching me about the blood amongst other things.

I am also thankful for Dr. Robert Ampiah Kwofi (Global Revival Ministries), Bishop Bob Asare (Faith Alive Ministries), Bishop Eric Ntorinkansah (Living Flames Baptist Church) for being dependable spiritual fathers.

Many thanks also go to Pas. David Oyedepo Jnr. (Winners Chapel, UK), Bishop Moses Owusu Sekyere, Rev. Grant Bulmuo (Fountain Gate Chapel UK), Rev. Emmanuel Anning and Dr. David Antwi (Kharis Chapel, UK) for the various mentorship roles they play in my life.

A great God bless you to Pas. Edward Obeng, Dr. Joshua Ofori and my other brothers, friends and loved ones in the ministry. I can't name you all but you know that I appreciate you dearly.

To all the ministers and members of Shine Ministries, London, God bless you for your loyalty and dedication over the years.

To my parents Rev. And Mrs G Aggrey-Solomon, thank you for raising me into someone who is being used by God. Mr and Mrs P D Quartey, thank you for giving me a wonderful wife.

To my wonderful wife, Selgelia and our miracle babies Judah and Tehillah, thank you for allowing me to work for Jesus and for helping me in all the ways you do.

One

BLOOD, ITS SIGNIFICANCE AND POWER

What is blood?

Blood is a word that draws all sorts of feelings to us humans. We all need blood to survive yet very few of us want to see blood. The colour of blood, red, is used in many cultures to represent danger or extreme seriousness. Blood is so important to us that very few of us are willing to donate it to even our loved ones in times of need.

I remember a time when my mother of blessed memory was so unwell that she needed blood to keep on living. A sister of hers touched by her predicament opted to go the hospital to donate the needed blood. Upon reaching the hospital however, the sheer fear of losing her own blood made her to change her mind.

She could not donate the promised blood even though all checks proved that she was fit and able to donate. My mother eventually passed on into glory but no one could blame my auntie because when it comes to blood we are talking about life. When a person gives blood, it is almost as giving his or her own life for another person's life. What then is blood and how much power is there in blood?

The Basic (Layman's) Science of Blood

According to scientists, "Blood is the body's liquid that gives us life."
(1) This means that without blood, there is no life. No living
organism can live without blood. Blood according to these scientists
is indispensable to life because of the following reasons:

1. It supplies oxygen and nutrients to our tissues. – The healthy
    human body is a complex combination of systems working
    together to achieve the common goal of healthy and purposeful
    living. These systems like the respiratory system are made up of
    organs and parts which are made up of tissues.
2. These tissues must be kept alive with the supply of oxygen and
    well with the supply of nutrients all the time so that they can keep
    the systems working to eventually keep the body well and alive.
    Blood is the vehicle which transports the much needed oxygen
    and nutrients to these tissues to enable them to keep functioning.
    Without blood, there will be no supply of oxygen and nutrients
    and the tissues will die, leading to the eventual death of that part,
    organ, or system of even the whole body.
3. It removes waste products. – When blood supplies our tissues
    with the much needed oxygen and nutrients, it does not return
    empty. It carries back the used oxygen which is now carbon
    dioxide as well as the residue of used nutrients and other toxins
    from various parts of the body and delivers them to the
    appropriate organs which eventually expel them out of the body.
    Without this vital function, the body will become poisoned from
    itself and illness or even death may occur.
4. It helps protect our body against attack by infection. Blood or
    better still, healthy blood is made up of red blood cells and white
    blood cells.
5. The job of the white blood cells is to fight every infection they
    meet anywhere in the body. Without blood therefore, infections
    will be free to grow anywhere in the body without any resistance
    and eventually destroy or kill the affected part or even the whole
    body.
6. It helps repair the body. – As we use our bodies in various
    activities, we experience wear and tear as it is with any other
    material substances. Some of the foods and drinks we consume

also create various problems for the body. There are also times when we injure the body through accidents or carelessness and other times on purpose as in surgical operations. Blood works in a wonderful way to bring the required healing materials to the affected part so as to heal or repair it. Without blood, wounds would not heal up and various breaches in the body would not be repaired.

7. It transports hormones. A hormone is a regulatory substance produced in an organism and transported in tissue fluids such as blood or sap to stimulate specific cells or tissues into action. This means that blood serves as the vehicle which transports the hormones to the various parts of the body to inform or prompt them into certain actions. Without blood therefore, hormones would not be transported and certain needed changes would not take place in our bodies.

8. It regulates the body's pH (acidity level) and temperature. The body or parts of the body have set levels of acidity and temperature for basic survival and also for specific functions. When the acidity or temperature level rises above or falls below the required level for effective operation or safe level for survival, there can be malfunction, illness or even death. Blood plays such an important role by working to keep the acidity and temperature levels in the various parts of the body at the required levels to keep us comfortable, functional, healthy and ultimately alive.

From the above, we can conclude that blood is so vital to our existence and so powerful as to determine whether we are comfortable or otherwise, functional or inoperative, healthy or sick, alive or dead.

We must do all we can to ensure that we have sufficient and healthy blood which is also able to circulate or travel through our bodies effectively. My basic advice here is to eat healthy, exercise regularly and have appropriate rest.

Why have we had to go through such a detailed albeit basic study of blood in a Christian book? You will be amazed to find out as we go along in this book that every knowledge of the function of the blood in the human body that we have, helps us to understand better the spiritual function of the precious blood of the Lamb of God in the life of a person who has chosen to hide his life in the precious blood of Jesus.

What Does the Bible Say About Blood?

We have just looked at the scientific relevance of blood. True science is always confirmed by the Bible. Science does not confirm the veracity of the Bible; the Bible confirms the veracity of science.

Science researches the truth about matter; the Bible is truth. It contains the truth about the living and the dead, the physical and spiritual, the past and the future. When the Bible declares a thing, it is not subject to proof by science; science only gains honour by catching up to the declared truth.

According to the Bible, blood is life. Before there was ever a laboratory, the word of God declared that blood is life. In the book of Deuteronomy, God tells His children to abstain from eating or drinking blood because "The blood is the life"

Deut. 12:23 - "Only be sure that thou eat not the blood: for the blood is the life; and thou mayest not eat the life with the flesh." –

In the first epistle of John, the beloved Apostle confirms the fact that blood is life by saying –

1 John 5:12 "He that hath the Son hath life; and he that hath not the Son of God hath not life."

This means that we only have life by having Jesus Christ the Son of God; but how do we have the Son? We have the Son only because of His shed blood as declared in Paul's letter to the Hebrews:

Heb. 9:22 - And almost all things are by the law purged with blood; and without shedding of blood is no remission.

Until blood is shed, there is no forgiveness and until there is forgiveness, there is no salvation and until there is salvation, there is no life. The Blood of Jesus therefore is the source of life to everyone who believes and receives it.

We can confidently say therefore that the Bible clearly equates blood to life. We who call ourselves Christians therefore claim to have "life" in the spirit because we have the only blood that works in the spiritual realm at work in our spirits. Our spirits have life or are alive because we have received "the blood of the spirit" and it is circulating effectively in our spiritual bodies. This healthy circulation evidently affects every aspect of our lives even in the physical because the physical is always governed by the spiritual.

This is why Jesus says that once He sets you free through His blood, albeit spiritual, you will be free in every area of your life. Spiritual freedom is the greatest freedom and spiritual life is the greatest life.

Now that we know what the bible says about the value of blood, let us look at how blood was used in the lives of our fathers in the Old Testament before Christ came. Let us look at how seriously they took the value of blood and how blood was used in various situation

Two

THE IMPORTANCE OF BLOOD IN THE OLD TESTAMENT

To appreciate the value of blood, it is important that we look at how it has been perceived and used right from the beginning of time. How did the fathers of old who heard first hand from God how they had to live their lives value blood? Let us go through the old testament scriptures to find some answers.

7 Uses of Blood in the Old Testament

1. **It was to be considered as the actual life of whatever it came from and was therefore not to be eaten or shed recklessly.**

2. The first evidence we have of man eating the meat of animals is after the Great flood of Noah's days. In Genesis chapter 9, we read about God asking Noah and his family to eat the meat of every moving thing upon the earth. In verse 4 however, God insist that man should not eat the meat if it still contained the blood. He describes the blood as the life.

   Gen. 9:4 - But flesh with the life thereof, which is the blood thereof, shall ye not eat. -

Later on in Deuteronomy chapter 12, we read again where God instructs His people not to eat meat which contained the blood nor eat or drink the blood itself. He states clearly that the blood is the life.

Deut. 12:23 - Only be sure that thou eat not the blood: for the blood is the life; and thou mayest not eat the life with the flesh.

Also because of the sacred nature of blood, it was not supposed to be shed recklessly, especially the blood of man. God made it clear that if anyone shed another man's blood, without reasonable cause, the offender's own blood was to be shed to compensate for the victim's blood.

Gen. 9:6 - Whoso sheddeth man's blood, by man shall his blood be shed: for in the image of God made he man.

This was why the people on Jonah's ship did all they could not to cast him into the sea. They actually had to pray for mercy before they cast him into the sea even though they knew he was the cause of their woes and that they had lost so much because of his disobedience and he had actually asked them to cast him into the sea. Blood was highly respected and not to be shed lightly at all.

Jonah 1:11-14 – 11Then said they unto him, What shall we do unto thee, that the sea may be calm unto us? for the sea wrought, and was tempestuous.
12And he said unto them, Take me up, and cast me forth into the sea; so shall the sea be calm unto you: for I know that for my sake this great tempest is upon you.
13Nevertheless the men rowed hard to bring it to the land; but they could not: for the sea wrought, and was tempestuous against them.
14Wherefore they cried unto the LORD, and said, We beseech thee, O LORD, we beseech thee, let us not perish for this man's life, and lay not upon us innocent blood: for thou, O LORD, hast done as it pleased thee.

God actually told Cain that he was cursed because he had wasted his brother's blood.

Gen. 4:11- And now art thou cursed from the earth, which hath opened her mouth to receive thy brother's blood from thy hand;

We can therefore conclude that blood was forbidden from being eaten or shed carelessly among God's people in the Old Testament. It was only good to be poured on the ground for a good reason.

3. It was used to cover the nakedness and curse of sin

The Bible says that immediately Adam and Eve ate the forbidden fruit, their eyes were opened and they found out that they were naked. Sin always removes the covering of God which is also known as the Presence of God. It is the Presence that gives us peace and joy.

It is the Presence that keeps us protected and empowered to make progress in life. When the Presence leaves, we become naked and empty.

Most of the times, we only try to fill that void or nakedness by seeking solace in other things that no dot really solve the problem but only mask them. They seek to hide our sensitivity to the actual effects of sin. Some of these things are alcohol, drugs, pornography, slandering, gluttony, excessive partying and the like. The sad truth from the use of these masks is that they actually eventually ruin our lives if we continue to indulge in them.

So Adam and Even tried to cover their nakedness or the emptiness that resulted from the departure of God's Presence by making clothes or coverings out of leaves. Can you imagine how long it was going to take before the leaves would wither and leave them naked again?

God in His mercy decided to give them a more lasting covering by shedding the blood of some animals. God could not get the skins from the animals without killing them. The wages of sin has always been death.

Every time a person commits sin, spiritual death occurs and it creates an imbalance in the spiritual realms. To balance the equation, there has to be a corresponding physical death by the perpetrator. Where this is not possible, an animal could be killed to defer the actual death sentence.

The blood of animals does not have a permanent atoning power for sins. They are only temporary even though last longer than that of plants.

God therefore gave them a temporary solution by killing animals in order to cover their nakedness with the skins.

Gen. 3:21 - Unto Adam also and to his wife did the LORD God make coats of skins, and clothed them.

What God did there was not just a mere physical covering, it had a spiritual significance. Spiritually, the blood that was spilled created a covering for Adam and Eve. This ordinance was confirmed for God's people as a continuous means of covering for their sins until such a time as the perfect lamb could be slain to break the power of the curse of sin forever.

Lev. 17:11 - For the life of a creature is in the blood, and I have given it to you to make atonement for yourselves on the altar; it is the blood that makes atonement for one's life.

Every time sin is committed, there has to be a corresponding shedding of blood. This remained an ordinance among God's people before the coming of the Messiah.

Heb.9:22 - And almost all things are by the law purged with blood; and without shedding of blood is no remission.

4. It was used to seal covenants

The Abrahamic Covenant - At the root of the Abrahamic covenant is the shedding of blood. This time it was not the blood of animals but the blood of the foreskin of all male children born to Abraham either as his own or born in his house.

The blood of the foreskin was used to seal the covenant that required Abraham to walk with God with a perfect and believing heart in return for God's protection, provision and enlargement.

Gen. 17:10-14 - This is my covenant, which ye shall keep, between me and you and thy seed after thee; Every man child among you shall be circumcised.

11And ye shall circumcise the flesh of your foreskin; and it shall be a token of the covenant betwixt me and you.

12And he that is eight days old shall be circumcised among you, every man child in your generations, he that is born in the house, or bought with money of any stranger, which is not of thy seed.

13He that is born in thy house, and he that is bought with thy money, must needs be circumcised: and my covenant shall be in your flesh for an everlasting covenant.

14And the uncircumcised man child whose flesh of his foreskin is not circumcised, that soul shall be cut off from his people; he hath broken my covenant. -

The National Covenant of Israel

When Moses brought the children of Israel out of Egypt, they had to covenant with God to walk in obedience to his ordinances. Moses read out all that God required of them and the children of Israel agreed to obey. After this agreement, Moses sprinkled blood upon the assembly to confirm the covenant.

Ex. 24:7-8 - And he took the book of the covenant, and read in the audience of the people: and they said, All that the LORD hath said will we do, and be obedient.

8And Moses took the blood, and sprinkled it on the people, and said, Behold the blood of the covenant, which the LORD hath made with you concerning all these words.

5. It was used to exempt one group of people from impending danger

After the display of persistent stubbornness from the Egyptian Pharaoh, God determined to play the last card in the bid to free His children Israel.

This last card involved the ultimate penalty of death; the death of the first born. The angel of death was going to pass through the nation in the night to kill every first born and the only thing that was to separate between those who were to die and those who were to live was blood. The angel of death would just pass on from any house that had the mark of the blood. Why didn't God ask for any other thing to be placed on the door posts other than blood?

Ex. 12:12-13 - For I will pass through the land of Egypt this night, and will smite all the firstborn in the land of Egypt, both man and beast; and against all the gods of Egypt I will execute judgment: I am the LORD.

13And the blood shall be to you for a token upon the houses where ye are: and when I see the blood, I will pass over you, and the plague shall not be upon you to destroy you, when I smite the land of Egypt. –

6. It was given as the ultimate sacrifice.

Women could lose their lives if they could not produce blood as proof of their virginity on their first encounter with their husbands.

Producing the blood of virginity was for those women a matter of life and death. A woman was therefore only going to give away that blood outside of marriage if she was willing to die for such a man. Her blood of virginity was therefore seen as the ultimate sacrifice. The man who took the virginity was bound to marry the woman because he had taken the ultimate sacrifice.

Deut. 22:13-21 - If any man takes a wife, and goes in unto her, and hates her,

14And give occasions of speech against her, and bring up an evil name upon her, and say, I took this woman, and when I came to her, I found her not a maid:

15Then shall the father of the damsel, and her mother, take and bring forth the tokens of the damsel's virginity unto the elders of the city in the gate:

16And the damsel's father shall say unto the elders, I gave my daughter unto this man to wife, and he hateth her;

17And, lo, he hath given occasions of speech against her, saying, I found not thy daughter a maid; and yet these are the tokens of my daughter's virginity. And they shall spread the cloth before the elders of the city.

18And the elders of that city shall take that man and chastise him;

19And they shall amerce him in an hundred shekels of silver, and give them unto the father of the damsel, because he hath brought up an evil name upon a virgin of Israel: and she shall be his wife; he may not put her away all his days.

20But if this thing be true, and the tokens of virginity be not found for the damsel:

21Then they shall bring out the damsel to the door of her father's house, and the men of her city shall stone her with stones that she die: because she hath wrought folly in Israel, to play the whore in her father's house: so shalt thou put evil away from among you. -

Deut. 22:28-29 - If a man find a damsel that is a virgin, which is not betrothed, and lay hold on her, and lie with her, and they be found;

29Then the man that lay with her shall give unto the damsel's father fifty shekels of silver, and she shall be his wife; because he hath humbled her, he may not put her away all his days.

The prophets of Baal cut themselves to implore him to send down fire

Another example of blood being used as the ultimate sacrifice was when the prophets of Baal were let down by the deity after a prolonged and persistent period of prayer for him to send down fire. Baal wouldn't or couldn't respond to their requests and Elijah kept taunting them.

Eventually, they resorted to cutting themselves till their blood gushed out. This, they did in the hope that upon seeing the ultimate sacrifice, Baal would hear them and answer their prayers and we all know how that story ended.

1 Kings 18:25-28 - And Elijah said unto the prophets of Baal, Choose you one bullock for yourselves, and dress it first; for ye are many; and call on the name of your gods, but put no fire under.

26And they took the bullock which was given them, and they dressed it, and called on the name of Baal from morning even until noon, saying, O Baal, hear us. But there was no voice, nor any that answered. And they leaped upon the altar which was made.

27And it came to pass at noon, that Elijah mocked them, and said, Cry aloud: for he is a god; either he is talking, or he is pursuing, or he is in a journey, or peradventure he sleepeth, and must be awaked.

28And they cried aloud, and cut themselves after their manner with knives and lancets, till the blood gushed out upon them. –

7. It was the most precious sacrifice before God

The bible says that there was a time when the sons of Adam were to give an offering unto God. Cain's offering was just fruits and crop produce. Most of the times, we are made to believe that the offering of Cain was just made up of rotten fruits. No it wasn't. They were good fruits but good is sometimes not just good enough. The offering of blood before God is always more precious than any other offering. That is why irrespective of what we can give towards the Kingdom of God, God is not really moved until we learn to give our lives. When blood is offered, a true offering has been given. God accepted both offerings, but he had more respect for Abel's offering because it was an offering of blood.

Gen. 4:3-5 - And in process of time it came to pass, that Cain brought of the fruit of the ground an offering unto the LORD.

4And Abel, he also brought of the firstlings of his flock and of the fat thereof. And the LORD had respect unto Abel and to his offering:

5But unto Cain and to his offering he had not respect. And Cain was very wroth, and his countenance fell.

On another occasion, the Bible says that King Solomon sacrificed so much blood that God appeared unto Him basically to ask Solomon for prayer requests. The sacrifice of blood is the most anyone can do and when it is done, God is always moved. It was so in the old testament and it is still so in the new testament albeit in a more blessed way.

2 Chron. 1:6-7- And Solomon went up thither to the brasen altar before the LORD, which was at the tabernacle of the congregation, and offered a thousand burnt offerings upon it. 7In that night did God appear unto Solomon, and said unto him, Ask what I shall give thee.

8.   It spoke either for or against the person who shed it

The people of the Old Testament knew of the power of the voice of blood.

Blood spoke then and it still speaks today. When people sacrificed blood, they expected the blood to speak for mercy or pardon for their sins. If it was an offering, they expected the blood to speak for favour upon their lives. Either way the blood had to speak. Consequently, if the blood was however shed acrimoniously, it was expected to speak against the offender. This was why the blood of the murderer was required to be shed in order to appease the voice of the blood which cried for justice. We see a good example of this in the book of Genesis, when Abel killed his brother out of bitterness.

Gen. 4:10-11 - And he said, What hast thou done? the voice of thy brother's blood crieth unto me from the ground.

11And now art thou cursed from the earth, which hath opened her mouth to receive thy brother's blood from thy hand; -

Three

THE BLOOD OF JESUS

Many people find it hard to appreciate why Christians put so much emphasis on the blood of Jesus. As far as they are concerned, blood is blood. This is however not the case when it comes to the blood of Jesus. It is so different from any other blood as we can see from the details below.

7 Things that distinguish the blood of Jesus from all other bloods

1. It is the most holy and most precious blood to be spilt on the earth

1 Pet. 1:18-19 - Forasmuch as ye know that ye were not redeemed with corruptible things, as silver and gold, from your vain conversation received by tradition from your fathers;

19But with the precious blood of Christ, as of a lamb without blemish and without spot:

In as much as we cannot input sin unto animals, we also know that they do not have any temptations to sin for which they must overcome. The blood of animals therefore cannot necessarily be called holy even if the animal is free of any blemishes.

Then we have the blood of other humans which have been spilt not necessarily because they committed any sins but either through the wickedness of others such as in the case of Abel or by accident. Such blood although innocent, can still not be called holy.

Throughout history, the only blood that was shed on earth which can be called holy is the blood of Jesus. Jesus did not commit any crime worthy of death, neither is there any record of Him committing any sin in His lifetime. His blood is therefore easily the most holy blood that ever touched the earth.

2. It is the only blood that permanently cries for mercy on earth and in Heaven

Heb. 12:24 - And to Jesus the mediator of the new covenant, and to the blood of sprinkling, that speaketh better things than that of Abel.

Anytime when innocent blood is shed, it either cries for mercy or for vengeance. The blood of animals although spoke for atonement, did not go far enough for total cleansing. This means that when an animal is sacrificed, there was always the need to sacrifice another for the next sin committed.

The blood of Abel and that of all people who have been innocently slain continue to cry for vengeance even if they are holy. In the book of Revelation, we actually hear of the Holy Martyrs, calling for the avenging of their blood.

Rev. 6:10 - And they cried with a loud voice, saying, How long, O Lord, holy and true, dost thou not judge and avenge our blood on them that dwell on the earth?

What a blessing therefore it is to know that the blood of Jesus is speaking better things for humanity, always crying for mercy and permanently covering our sins.

3. It is the only blood that was willingly offered for the redemption of another

John 10:17-18 - Therefore doth my Father love me, because I lay down my life, that I might take it again.

18No man taketh it from me, but I lay it down of myself. I have power to lay it down, and I have power to take it again. This commandment have I received of my Father.

Of all the blood that has been shed since creation, none has been done willingly. Even criminals do all they can to avoid death. The animals used for sacrifice do not do so willingly.

Christ however laid down His life as the Bible says even before the foundations of the earth were laid. And when the appointed time came, He willingly came from heaven to earth, gave up His God nature, put on the nature of man, endured all temptations, healed the sick, raised the dead and ultimately laid down His life in the most dishonourable way just so you and I could be saved. No one forced Him to die, He died willingly. When Peter tried to fight for Him, He prevented him, saying if He wanted to defend Himself. He could call for legions of angels but He declined to do so. O what a lovely saviour.

4. It is the only blood that broke the captivity of Satan permanently.

The death of Christ and the shedding of His blood brokered a permanent deliverance for humanity from the captivity of Satan. This was done in 5 ways as recorded in *Matt. 27:45, 50-54.*

a. The hidden darkness was revealed

Matt. 27:45 - Now from the sixth hour there was darkness over all the land unto the ninth hour.

We live in a very evil world where satanic activities are rife.

The unfortunate thing however is that this evil is often covered with fake light, deceiving many people and making them not live carefully. The Bible says that Satan parades himself as an angel of light. The blood of Jesus however uncovers him and his cohorts. The shed blood of Jesus reveals all hidden darkness no matter how it is disguised.

b. The veil that kept the ordinary from the holy was torn apart. All can become holy.

Matt. 27:50-51 - Jesus, when he had cried again with a loud voice, yielded up the ghost.

51And, behold, the veil of the temple was rent in twain from the top to the bottom; and the earth did quake, and the rocks rent;

With the renting of the veil, all can be holy through the shed blood of Jesus. It amazes me when we go out for soul winning and people say, "Well I'm not holy enough" then we tell them, that's exactly why He came. With the shed blood, we can all become holy, we can all become priests, and we can all become the sons of God. Hallelujah!

c. The foundations of satanic dominion was shaken apart

Matt. 27:50-51 - Jesus, when he had cried again with a loud voice, yielded up the ghost...........; and the earth did quake, and the rocks rent;

Adam sold the earth to the devil through the sin of Eden. All through our history after that, Satan has held control over the earth.

He told Jesus during His temptation that everything on earth had been given to him and that he had the right to give it to whoever he wanted.

The blood of Jesus however wrestled the control of the earth from the devil's hands on that glorious day. Everyone who believes in Him therefore can walk in total dominion on earth.

In John 10:10, Jesus, said the thief only came to steal, kill and destroy but He had come that we might have life and have it more abundantly. Yes, the blood of Jesus empowers us to reign in the earth. He has made us royal priests. Hallelujah!

d. Strongholds that kept men in bondage was broken up

Matt. 27:50-51 - Jesus, when he had cried again with a loud voice, yielded up the ghost. And, behold...... the rocks rent;

The blood of Jesus also gives us the power over curses, sins and addictions that easily destroy destinies. The hard places of life, the things one cannot easily overcome naturally are now made easy by the shedding of the precious blood of Jesus. Yes, you can stop that sin. Yes that curse that has tormented your life and that of your family over the generations can be broken. Yes, you can be healed. Every hard thing in your life can be turned around by the blood of

Jesus.

e. The graves that kept holy men in captivity were opened, empowering them to live again.

Matt. 27: 52-54 - And the graves were opened; and many bodies of the saints which slept arose,

53And came out of the graves after his resurrection, and went into the holy city, and appeared unto many.

54Now when the centurion, and they that were with him, watching Jesus, saw the earthquake, and those things that were done, they feared greatly, saying, Truly this was the Son of God.

Many people try in their own strength to live godly and holy lives but as hard as they try, they easily end up disappointed with one sin after the other. Many want to live a holy life but they just can't practice it. Many are saints at heart but they are spiritually locked up in graves that prevent them from living the saintly life freely.

The Bible says that the Son of God was revealed for this purpose that He may destroy the works of the devil. Through the blood of Jesus, you can live a fully functional life of holiness and righteousness. The blood will set you free from any spiritual grave. Glory to God!

5. It is the only blood that can wash away the sins of mankind

Rev. 1:5 - And from Jesus Christ, who is the faithful witness, and the first begotten of the dead, and the prince of the kings of the earth. Unto him that loved us, and washed us from our sins in his own blood,

The hymn writer wrote "What can wash away my sin, nothing but the blood of Jesus". The blood of animals only atone for a moment, the blood of other men only cry for vengeance but the blood of Jesus washes away every sin, no matter the gravity.

No matter what sin you have committed, the blood of Jesus is still cleansing. Come to Him now and see how clean you can become.

6. It is the only blood that came back to life

Rev. 1:18 - I am he that liveth, and was dead; and, behold, I am alive for evermore, Amen; and have the keys of hell and of death.

Acts 2:24 - Whom God hath raised up, having loosed the pains of death: because it was not possible that he should be holden of it.

Isn't it amazing to be serving the living God? All other gods are dead but our Jesus even after shedding His precious blood on Calvary's cross , is alive never to die again but to live forever more. Hallelujah, Jesus is alive and the blood that was shed for our sins is alive and at work for the redeemed. Whosoever wills, may come to the living blood of Jesus.

7. It is the only blood that gives eternal life

John 6:52-54 - The Jews therefore strove among themselves, saying, How can this man give us his flesh to eat?

53Then Jesus said unto them, Verily, verily, I say unto you, Except ye eat the flesh of the Son of man, and drink his blood, ye have no life in you.

54Whoso eateth my flesh, and drinketh my blood, hath eternal life; and I will raise him up at the last day.

The blood of Jesus is the only blood that assures us of life beyond the grave. When you take cover under the blood of Jesus, you're safe indeed. Other bloods may only promise temporary relief but the blood of Jesus stands forever for our redemption.

Just as Jesus said, except you're covered by His blood, you have no hope. Our only hope is in the blood. Come to Jesus for eternal life and if you're already in Christ, rest assured, your eternity is safe. Glory to God!

Four

THE BLOOD OF JESUS IN THE BODY OF CHRIST (THE CHURCH)

It will interest you to know that there are striking similarities between what blood does to the natural body and what the blood of Jesus does to the body of Christ. It is not for nothing that the church is called the body of Christ.

If we are the body of Christ, then the blood of Jesus will flow through us and if it flows through us, it will certainly have an impact just as blood affects the body.

The blood flowing through the body of Christ will dsitribute grace where it is needed, it will purge the body from sin and demonic infections, it will repair hurts and issues that bring sorrow and discouragement, it will keep people from different natural backgrounds together as one family and it will help keep us all in check so none goes astray into any extremes. The blood is still at work in the church. Lets see how.

The 6 Scientific Uses of Blood and how they exemplify the Uses of the blood of Jesus in the body of Christ

1. **Just as blood transports nutrients into the parts of the body, the blood of Jesus draws grace and gifts from God and**

releases them to the body of Christ

Eph. 4:8 - Wherefore he saith, When he ascended up on high, he led captivity captive, and gave gifts unto men.

After purchasing us with His blood, the Bible says that Jesus is still releasing gifts and grace unto the body of Christ here on earth. These graces and gifts empower our Christian living and make the experience so real and profound. Without the active work of the blood of Jesus, Christianity is dull and dead.

This is why Christians and the churches must actively engage the blood of Jesus for continuous victory.

2. Blood eliminates waste and toxins from the system just as the blood of Jesus purges the body of Christ from sin.

Heb. 2:11- For both he that sanctifieth and they who are sanctified are all of one: for which cause he is not ashamed to call them brethren,

1 John 1:1 - But if we walk in the light, as he is in the light, we have fellowship one with another, and the blood of Jesus Christ his Son cleanseth us from all sin.

The sanctification work of the blood of Jesus is not just a one off work, it is continuous. After washing our sins away at salvation, the blood continues to work on a daily basis, cleansing us of all the little and even big sins we commit daily, knowingly or unknowingly. This is what keeps us in perpetual fellowship with a Holy God.

We know that sin is spiritual infection that causes sickness, failure and even death but as the blood of Jesus continues to cleanse us, we are kept rejuvenated and healthy all the time in the Lord.

3. Blood fights infections just as the blood of Jesus fights and destroys demonic contamination or activity among believers.

1 John 3:8 - He that committeth sin is of the devil; for the devil sinneth from the beginning. For this purpose the Son of God was manifested, that he might destroy the works of the devil.

Through the blood of Jesus, every satanic attack or activity against God's children is arrested and destroyed. The blood of Jesus serves as an antivirus protection for the saints. We are thus covered permanently.

Anytime you sense satanic activity of any kind in your life, family or church, just invoke the power in the blood of Jesus and see the victory come immediately.

4. Blood helps repair the body just as the blood of Jesus brings healing where there are physical, emotional or spiritual hurts in the body of Christ.

Heb. 2:14-15 – For as much then as the children are partakers of flesh and blood, he also himself likewise took part of the same; that through death he might destroy him that had the power of death, that is, the devil;

15 And deliver them who through fear of death were all their lifetime subject to bondage.

Without the repairing ability of the blood, a person will live in constant fear of infections. This is because the next infection could be the one which kills as in the case of people who are infected with the HIV virus. This virus weakens the blood's ability to fight infections as well as repair broken cells or tissues. This makes every hurt or infection, a potential death sentence.

The blood of Jesus however breaks that bondage and effectively repairs every breach in our bodies, souls and spirits and even in entire churches and in the whole body of Christ, bring us back into the place of wholeness.

5. It carries hormones to parts of the body just as the blood of Jesus unifies different peoples and nationalities into one people called body of Christ.

Rev. 5:9-10 - And they sung a new song, saying, Thou art worthy to take the book, and to open the seals thereof: for thou was slain, and hast redeemed us to God by thy blood out of every kindred, and tongue, and people, and nation;

10 And hast made us unto our God kings and priests: and we shall reign on the earth.

Hormones help the body to live in conformity. The various seasons of life and situations are communicated as hormones to all parts of the body to ensure that the whole body functions as one. These hormones are carried to all parts of the body by the blood.

In the same way, the blood of Jesus is the only blood that is able to bring together, people from all nationalities and backgrounds and make them into one body called the body of Christ.

It is beautiful when you visit some churches and see people from diverse races and socio-cultural backgrounds worshiping together in love and unity. That is what the blood can do.

6. It acts as a thermostat to regulate the body temperature just as the blood of Jesus covers the natural differences and extremes among God's people and brings them to the common place called a people "Redeemed by the blood"

Rev. 7:9 - After this I beheld, and, lo, a great multitude, which no man could number, of all nations, and kindreds, and people, and tongues, stood before the throne, and before the Lamb, clothed with white robes, and palms in their hands;

Blood serves as a regulator of body temperature. Where it is too hot or cold, blood works to bring that part in sync with the general body temperature. This ensures that the body is kept together and in health.

The blood of Jesus equally functions as the equaliser to the body of Christ. Many people believe that Christians are all too diverse with very different theological perspectives and congregational practices but when all is said and done, there is one thing that is the most important determinant of who we are. It is the blood of Jesus.

We are not going to Heaven because we believe in tongues or not. It is not about whether we should clap in a service or not. It is not even about what day we must keep as the Sabbath. When all is said and done, when we stand before the Master, the only thing that will matter is, whether we are washed in the blood of the Lamb or not. Hallelujah.

$\mathcal{F}ive$

THE BLOOD OF JESUS FULFILS EVERY OLD TESTAMENT DEMAND

The blood of Jesus answers every demand for blood for the sins of mankind. His blood is the summation of everything we will need to be free from sin and its repercussions.

The 7 Fold sprinkling of the Old Testament blood and it's replication through the suffering and death of Christ.

Lev. 16:14 - And he shall take of the blood of the bullock, and sprinkle it with his finger upon the mercy seat eastward; and before the mercy seat shall he sprinkle of the blood with his finger seven times.

God instructed the priests of the Old Testament as to how they must apply or sprinkle the blood of the atonement. He stated specifically that it had to be sprinkled seven times. Amazingly, Jesus was also made to shed His blood in seven different places in His redemption work for humanity.

1. At Gethsemane – He sweated blood

Luke 22:44 - And being in an agony he prayed more earnestly: and his sweat was as it were great drops of blood falling down to the ground.

The first place where Jesus shed His blood was in the Garden of Gethsemane. The Bible says that He prayed and found Himself in so much agony that His sweat dropped as blood.

2. They slapped His face and pulled His facial hair

Mark 14:65 - And some began to spit on him, and to cover his face, and to buffet him, and to say unto him, Prophesy: and the servants did strike him with the palms of their hands.

Is. 50:6 - I gave my back to the smiters, and my cheeks to them that plucked off the hair: I hid not my face from shame and spitting.

The second place where Jesus shed His blood was when they slapped Him and pulled His hair. It is believed that when they slapped Jesus' face and pulled out the hair from His face, there was the shedding of blood. This is very consistent with how any normal human body would react to the violent slapping of the face by wild and aggressive soldiers. It is not unusual also that when a person's facial hairs are pulled out by force, there will be blood.

3. The Crown of Thorns on His head

Matt. 27:29 - And when they had platted a crown of thorns, they put it upon his head, and a reed in his right hand: and they bowed the knee before him, and mocked him, saying, Hail, King of the Jews!

Jesus shed His blood for the third time when they put the crown of thorns on His head. The crown of thorns they put on Jesus' head naturally pierced His skin and even His skull. This caused a lot of bleeding as scientist confirms that head injuries usually do cause a lot of bleeding.

4. His back was beaten till the skin was torn

John 19:1 - Then Pilate therefore took Jesus, and scourged him.
Is. 50:6 - I gave my back to the smiters, ...

Fourthly, Jesus shed His blood through His back as they scourged Him with the thirty nine strokes of the crudest whips ever invented. Historical accounts have it that the skin on His back was totally destroyed, engendering profuse bleeding.

5. His hands were pierced and nailed on the cross

John 20:20 - And when he had so said, he shewed unto them his hands ....

For the fifth time Jesus shed His blood when they put Him on the cross and nailed his hands to the wood. Each hand was nailed to either side of the cross causing bleeding from both hands.

6. His feet were nailed to the cross

Luke 24:40 - And when he had thus spoken, he shewed them ...... his feet.

Jesus shed His blood for the sixth time on the cross when they nailed His feet to the wood. Both feet were nailed to the vertical beam causing more bleeding from the gentle saviour. It is worth noting also that the nails used in those times where not as refined as the ones we have today. Those were some very crude nails of irregular shape and hardly smooth.

7. They pierced His side

John 19:34 - But one of the soldiers with a spear pierced his side, and forthwith came there out blood and water.

The seventh and final place where Jesus shed His blood was when the soldiers wanted to confirm that He was truly dead. This was because they wanted to bury the crucified early enough to make way for the high Sabbath. The two thieves crucified with Him were not dead yet and they had to break their legs to quicken their death.

They were however quite shocked to find that Jesus had already died, forgetting that having shed so much blood, he had very little to live on, the same of which could not be said of the thieves.

To confirm that Jesus was dead and fulfil the levitical commandment of the seven fold sprinkling of the blood of atonement therefore, they pierced His side and there was a gushing out of water and blood.

Six

THE BLOOD OF JESUS CANCELS THE CURSE OF EDEN

God does not do anything for the sake of doing it. Everything He does has a reason and the same is the case with the shedding of Jesus' blood. Every point where Jesus shed his blood was for the cancellation of a particular curse imposed on humanity through the high treason of Adam and Eve in the garden of Eden.

We know that when man sinned, he lost God's Presence and was also placed under a curse. In John 10:10, Jesus says the thief only came to kill, steal and destroy but that He had come to give us abundant life. Jesus therefore is the cancellation of the curse on humanity. This He did through the shedding of His blood.

The Implications of the 7 ways in which Christ shed His blood

1. The agonising sweat of blood in the Garden of Gethsemane replaced the curse of surviving by the sweat of the face in Genesis Chapter 3

Gen. 3:19 - In the sweat of thy face shalt thou eat bread, till thou return unto the ground; ...

After the fall of man, God placed this curse that mankind would only survive through the struggles of life. When Jesus agonised in prayer however, His precious blood replaced that curse and we are now free to live a struggle free life. You can succeed without undue struggle. Life under Christ is not supposed to be a painful struggle any more. Thank God for Jesus.

2. The slapping of His face and the pulling of His facial hair replaces all the curses of sorrow

Gen. 3:16-17 - Unto the woman he said, I will greatly multiply thy sorrow and thy conception; in sorrow thou shalt bring forth children; and thy desire shall be to thy husband, and he shall rule over thee.

17And unto Adam he said, Because thou hast hearkened unto the voice of thy wife, and hast eaten of the tree, of which I commanded thee, saying, Thou shalt not eat of it: cursed is the ground for thy sake; in sorrow shalt thou eat of it all the days of thy life;

After the fall of man, both the woman and the man were cursed to a life of sorrow. Sorrow is mostly shown in the face but Jesus offered His face for every pain so that we can be free. As they slapped His face, the curse of tears and sorrow were being cancelled. As they pulled off His hair, our tears were being washed away. You can now live a life without sorrow because of what Jesus has done. Hallelujah!

3. The crown of thorns replaces the chastisement of our peace.

Is. 53:5 - But he was wounded for our transgressions, he was bruised for our iniquities: the chastisement of our peace was upon him; and with his stripes we are healed.

Gen. 3:8-10 - And they heard the voice of the LORD God walking in the garden in the cool of the day: and Adam and his wife hid themselves from the presence of the LORD God amongst the trees of the garden.

9And the LORD God called unto Adam, and said unto him, Where art thou?

10And he said, I heard thy voice in the garden, and I was afraid, because I was naked; and I hid myself.

Sin always results in fear and anxiety. Adam and Eve were not exempted from this phenomenon. Immediately they sinned, they saw that they were naked and they became afraid. They panicked and lost their peace. Depression, mental instabilities of all kinds stem from this incidence. Sin breaks down our peace. When God came looking, Adam went hiding.

Jesus however kindly accepted the crown of thorns on His precious head so that we who come to Him may have our peace restored. He is our prince of Peace, the pains for the price of our peace was put on Him. In Christ, you are assured true peace.

4. The stripes on His back and the tearing of His skin covered our skins from (sin) nakedness and the sicknesses (wages) that result from the nakedness gets healed

Gen. 3:10 - And he said, I heard thy voice in the garden, and I was afraid, because I was naked; and I hid myself.

Gen. 3:21 - Unto Adam also and to his wife did the LORD God make coats of skins, and clothed them.

1 Pet. 2:24 - Who his own self bare our sins in his own body on the tree that we, being dead to sins, should live unto righteousness: by whose stripes ye were healed.

The wages of sin have always been death. When man sinned, they immediately saw that he was naked and needed a covering. God had to kill an animal to make clothes for them even though that was not as permanent as it could be. Christ offered His back to be beaten in order to give us all a permanent spiritual covering, making us holy again, restoring the presence and restoring all health back to us. In Christ, you are no longer naked because of the blood.

5. The piercing of His hands reverses the curse of fruitlessness

Gen. 3:18 - Thorns also and thistles shall it bring forth to thee; and thou shalt eat the herb of the field;

After the curse, man was condemned to a life of struggles and poverty. The earth was cursed in such a way that man would work so hard and get so little for reward. When Jesus shed His blood in His hands however, that curse of poverty and fruitlessness was broken forever and the blessing of fruitfulness in Genesis 1:28 was restored. In Christ, through His blood, you are now free to prosper.

6. **The piercing of His feet reverses the curse on the feet that were supposed to wander when man was kicked out of the Garden. We are now free to return to the garden**

Gen. 3:23-24 - Therefore the LORD God sent him forth from the garden of Eden, to till the ground from whence he was taken. So he drove out the man; and he placed at the east of the garden of Eden Cherubims, and a flaming sword which turned every way, to keep the way of the tree of life.

David said, he had his contentment in the Presence of the Lord and he is no different from any of us. We all can only prosper when we are in God's Presence. When man sinned however, as part of the curse, he was driven out of the garden, from the Presence of God.

Man therefore was to live as a fatherless vagabond. This accounts for why many people cannot hold on to one thing till it succeeds. Many people are under this curse and they keep trying one thing or one person after the other either in business or even in marriage.

Thank God however for Jesus. As they pierced His feet, the curse of the vagabond was broken.

Through the blood of Jesus therefore, you can have stability on all you do as you camp in His Presence. Glory!

7. **The piercing of His side to confirm His death reverses the proclamation of death and confirms life once again to the believer.**

Gen. 3:19b – "for dust thou art, and unto dust shalt thou return."

John 11:25-26 - Jesus said unto her, I am the resurrection, and the life: he that believeth in me, though he were dead, yet shall he live: And whosoever liveth and believeth in me shall never die. Believest thou this?

Jesus died that we might have life. If we put our trust in Him, His death will replace ours and our death will only be a transition from the earth into His eternal Presence. His word is true. In Him we have eternal life. He died and rose again just to confirm to us that we can also live again all because of what His blood has done for us. What an amazing grace.

Seven

HOW TO BENEFIT FROM THE BLOOD OF JESUS

The Application of the Blood

We have learnt so far a lot about the power, provisions and liberty we have in the blood of Jesus Christ our Lord and saviour. It is however not enough to just know about the blood without knowing how to apply it to real life situations. The things of the Kingdom are not just for head knowledge but for the transformation of our lives which comes about only by appropriate application.

The testimonies that have resulted in the application of the blood of Jesus have been amazing and too many to count. I would not be writing this book if I had not experienced the power in the application of blood of Jesus. You must understand one thing; the blood will not benefit you until you make use of it.

James 1:22 - But be ye doers of the word, and not hearers only, deceiving your own selves.

1. The Conditions for applying the blood

There are three major conditions for putting the blood of Jesus to use. These conditions apply whether you need the blood to work for yourself, family, friends, ministry, community or nation.

a. You have to be born again –

Until your sins are forgiven by God through the blood of Jesus, the Bible says that your prayers are even an abomination unto God. Until you are born again, you cannot use the blood of Jesus to your advantage because you do not qualify.

The blood of Jesus only works for those who have had their sins forgiven and have been washed in the blood of the lamb. These are those who have sincerely accepted Jesus Christ as their Lord and personal saviour through prayer in faith.

You can also become born again if you can believe that Jesus Christ is God who became man and lived a sinless life and gave his life in substitution for yours. If you can then pray and ask Him to forgive all of your sins and become your Lord for the rest of your life and if you can confess Him as your Lord to others, you will be born again and will have the right to use the blood of Jesus to your advantage.

Pro. 15:8 - The sacrifice of the wicked is an abomination to the LORD: but the prayer of the upright is his delight.

b. You need Faith

The second condition necessary for the effective application of the blood of Jesus is Faith.

Eph. 2:8 - For by grace are ye saved through faith; and that not of yourselves: it is the gift of God:

The blood of Jesus is available to us and still remains powerful even in our generation. The problem we have however is that it does not sound very modern or 21st century. Many Christians therefore wanting to look trendy or modern abandon this all powerful provision in favour of basic and powerless Christian living which only depends on head knowledge.

Christianity is a life of power not theories and if this power will come alive for you, you need faith. You need enough boldness to go beyond popular opinion and your own sensitivity in order to get hold of what God has for you. Bishop David Oyedepo has a favourite saying "It is foolishness to be shameful of that which is gainful".

If you need breakthroughs, if you need power, if you need victory, forget about your nerves and step out boldly to apply the blood. The results will always justify your step of faith. Don't suffer while hiding behind diplomacy. Get up and act.

c. **You need Holiness** – walking worthy of our calling or profession.

1 Cor. 11:27-32 - Wherefore whosoever shall eat this bread, and drink this cup of the Lord, unworthily, shall be guilty of the body and blood of the Lord.

28But let a man examine himself, and so let him eat of that bread, and drink of that cup.

29For he that eateth and drinketh unworthily, eateth and drinketh damnation to himself, not discerning the Lord's body.

30For this cause many are weak and sickly among you, and many sleep.

31For if we would judge ourselves, we should not be judged.

32But when we are judged, we are chastened of the Lord, that we should not be condemned with the world.

I don't want to sound judgemental here and of course our holiness is all in Christ. You don't have to be perfect to use the blood of Jesus otherwise no one would qualify. You however must be very careful not to use it as something common. You cannot use the blood in inappropriate language for example; neither can you use it when you are wilfully living in or committing sins.

You can however use it to break free from sinful habits or the like.

The blood of Jesus must not be trampled upon. Use it with respect.

2. The Communion, The Sprinkling and The Confession - 3 Main Ways of Applying the Blood

First of all, you must understand that using the blood of Jesus is mainly symbolic through faith. We do not have the actual blood of Jesus but through faith, we can use various liquids for example to represent it just as Jesus demonstrated to His disciples on the last supper. Where no actual substance is required you can only speak it by faith and it will still work. All you need is faith.

There are three major ways in which to use the blood of Jesus. You can use the blood through taking of the communion. You can also use it through symbolical sprinkling. You can again use the blood of Jesus in confessional (prayer and faith proclamations) declarations.

Eight

BENEFITING FROM THE BLOOD OF JESUS THROUGH
THE COMMUNION

The Communion – Christ instituted the communion Himself.

The communion involves the use of grape juice or any appropriate juice and bread. The type of "elements" used is not as important as the faith with which you take it.

It is normally taken with the reading of the scriptures below or similar ones which give account of Jesus' last supper with His disciples. From the scripture we can infer that the bread is eaten first before the drink.

Matt. 26:26-28 - And as they were eating, Jesus took bread, and blessed it, and brake it, and gave it to the disciples, and said, Take, eat; this is my body.

27And he took the cup, and gave thanks, and gave it to them, saying, Drink ye all of it;

28For this is my blood of the new testament, which is shed for many for the remission of sins.

The Significance of the Communion

1. Redemption

One major thing to stand on when you take the communion is to know that it represents our redemption from the Old Testament which is the law. As we all know, no one could keep the law so it turned out to be a curse for us. The use of the blood therefore enforces our stand in the new covenant, giving us the power through the blood to reject every curse which is a result of the law. The blood enforces the forgiveness of all our sins, making us Holy and positioned for God's blessings instead of the curse. It helps us to enforce our position that Christ has redeemed us from the curse of the law.

1 Cor. 11:23-26 - For I have received of the Lord that which also I delivered unto you, That the Lord Jesus the same night in which he was betrayed took bread:

24 And when he had given thanks, he brake it, and said, Take, eat: this is my body, which is broken for you: this do in remembrance of me.

25 After the same manner also he took the cup, when he had supped, saying, This cup is the new testament in my blood: this do ye, as oft as ye drink it, in remembrance of me.

26 For as often as ye eat this bread, and drink this cup, ye do shew the Lord's death till he come.

2. Consciousness of Being New Creation

The communion is also to help keep us in perpetual consciousness that Christ has died for us and that we are saved. This consciousness gives us the overcomers' mentality and helps us not to settle for any sort of satanic encroachment over our lives. He died that we might have life. We must therefore reject anything that does not look like life in our lives through the blood in the communion.

John 6.53-57 - Then Jesus said unto them, Verily, verily, I say unto you, Except ye eat the flesh of the Son of man, and drink his blood, ye have no life in you.

54 Whoso eateth my flesh, and drinketh my blood, hath eternal life; and I will raise him up at the last day.

55 For my flesh is meat indeed, and my blood is drink indeed.

56 He that eateth my flesh, and drinketh my blood, dwelleth in me, and I in him.

57 As the living Father hath sent me, and I live by the Father: so he that eateth me, even he shall live by me.

3. Unity with Christ

The communion also brings us into unity with Christ. When we take it, we are spiritually connected with Him enabling us to draw all needed virtues from Him whilst like dialysis, He drains our systems of all toxins and infections. What a blessing.

John 6: 56-57 - He that eateth my flesh, and drinketh my blood, dwelleth in me, and I in him.

57As the living Father hath sent me, and I live by the Father: so he that eateth me, even he shall live by me.

4. The Release of Power

There is a great release of power when we take the communion. There are numerous testimonies of healings, marital and business breakthroughs among others that have taken place after people took the communion. Churches and families must take the communion regularly for the release of the power in the blood into their own lives.

The Administration of the Communion

One may ask how often we have to take the communion or whether we must take it only at church. The answer is right up there in the scriptures. We are commanded to take it as often as possible. You can even take it daily. I actually know many people who take it daily. Also you don't need to wait till you are in church. You are a royal priesthood. You can pray over it, standing on the appropriate scriptures by faith and take it. Any good drink, any good bread can be used so start now.

Nine

BENEFITING FROM THE BLOOD OF JESUS THROUGH SPRINKLING

Sprinkling or Physical Application Of The Blood – (Please Note that this is only done symbolically)

The sprinkling of the blood is another way through which we can benefit from the blood of Jesus. This I know is not a very popular thing to do but I have seen many instant miracles through it. I am not declaring it as a must do but if you have faith, you can see the power of God through its use. Just as in the anointing with oil, the oil itself has no healing properties but still works because it is done backed by the prayer of faith, so does the sprinkling of the blood work.

Application

You only need any juice (or even water) that you would have used for the communion for sprinkling. You don't have to go about making everything wet. You only need a little. What counts is the faith you use to declare that whatever object you are sprinkling is being sanctified by the blood of Jesus.

Let us look at a few examples in scripture where blood was

sprinkled.

1. For protection and exemption from impending danger

Ex. 12:21-23 - Then Moses called for all the elders of Israel, and said unto them, Draw out and take you a lamb according to your families, and kill the passover.

22And ye shall take a bunch of hyssop, and dip it in the blood that is in the bason, and strike the lintel and the two side posts with the blood that is in the bason; and none of you shall go out at the door of his house until the morning.

23For the LORD will pass through to smite the Egyptians; and when he seeth the blood upon the lintel, and on the two side posts, the LORD will pass over the door, and will not suffer the destroyer to come in unto your houses to smite you.

This is where the Jews were commanded to sprinkle blood upon their doors to protect them from the angel of death who was being sent to kill every first born of Egypt. The blood gave them exemption. If the blood of animals could give them exemption then, then the blood of Jesus, sprinkled through faith will give us even better exemption and protection from every danger.

2. For breakthrough

Heb. 12:24 - And to Jesus the mediator of the new covenant, and to the blood of sprinkling, that speaketh better things than that of Abel.

The blood that Jesus sprinkled for us, continues to speak good things for us. Whenever you need a breakthrough, you can stand on this scripture and activate the sprinkling for your good.

3. For consecration

Lev. 8:23 - And he slew it; and Moses took of the blood of it, and put it upon the tip of Aaron's right ear, and upon the thumb of his right hand, and upon the great toe of his right foot.

Another way in which the blood of Jesus is used is for the consecration of God's servants. This is done by applying the blood or whatever is being used as a symbol to the right ear, the right thumb and the right toe.

The blood is applied to the right ear to protect the minister's ears and mind from the voice of the enemy. The enemy's voice can easily mislead God's servant who can in turn mislead God's people. It also quickens the minister's ears to the voice of the Lord which is the most important voice in the work of the Lord.

The blood is also applied to the right thumb to enforce sanctification on the servant of God's actions. If we must lead by example, our actions must be good enough to emulate. Paul said, imitate me as I imitate Christ. The blood on the thumb also empowers God's minister to do what God commands him to do. The work of God cannot be done with feeble hands.

The final place where the blood is applied is on the great right toe. This is done to protect the walk of God's minister. It protects his feet from going to the wrong place. It also empowers the minister to take steps or go where God wants him to. It gives dominion and spiritual authority where the minister treads.

Before you pass it as a sole preserve of men of God, don't forget that you are also called into the work of God as a Christian. In the New Testament, we are all called to advance God's Kingdom through soul winning, soul strengthening and soul establishing. You are also a minister. Sanctify and empower your ears, thumbs and toes for the work of God. Don't forget this is all symbolic and is done only through faith. Without faith, it will only become a weird and mundane ritual which you must avoid.

4. To build a hedge of protection

I believe that that the blood of Jesus can be used by faith to demarcate places where the enemy cannot cross. Once during a deliverance session, I was led to make such a demarcation after we had struggled for some time with the exercise. I sensed that the demon was communicating with other external powers which kept her recharging. Immediately, the demarcation was made, the demon became isolated and powerless, enabling us to drive it out a lot quickly.

From scripture, there is evidence that God can set a hedge of protection around people, houses, families, possessions and properties, endeavours and businesses as well as around one's influence.

If He did that for people in the Old Testament, what makes us think that He cannot do the same for us through the blood of Jesus by faith. Don't forget that it is not the sprinkling that initiates the protection. It has already been made available for you. You only activate your faith to connect with the provision through the sprinkling.

Eccl. 10:8 - He that diggeth a pit shall fall into it; and whoso breaketh an hedge, a serpent shall bite him.

From this scripture, we can infer that hedges are made for our protection and when they are not handled properly, there can be unpleasant consequences. Keep God's hedge over your life. Live a holy life but also keep activating the hedge through the blood by faith.

Job 1.4-5 - And his sons went and feasted in their houses, everyone his day; and sent and called for their three sisters to eat and to drink with them.

5And it was so, when the days of their feasting were gone about, that Job sent and sanctified them, and rose up early in the morning, and offered burnt offerings according to the number of them all: for Job said, It may be that my sons have sinned, and cursed God in their hearts. Thus did Job continually.

Job. 1.9-10 - Then Satan answered the LORD, and said, Doth Job fear God for nought?

10Hast not thou made an hedge about him, and about his house, and about all that he hath on every side? thou hast blessed the work of his hands, and his substance is increased in the land.

Holiness is extremely important for God's hedge of protection to work. Do not break your hedge by your actions as you activate it through the blood by faith.

Ten

BENEFITING FROM THE BLOOD OF JESUS THROUGH
CONFESSIONS

Confessional use

The power of the blood is known only to the redeemed of the Lord. Until a person is saved or has made the first confession of Jesus Christ as Lord, he has no right to use the blood of Jesus in his confessions.

By confessional use of the blood, I mean you can and must declare your freedom in Christ through the blood. This can be done in prayer, in basic conversations or through faith declarations. In all cases, the confessor must make the declaration in faith. We have seen demons leave people just because they were able to say something, "I accept Jesus Christ as my Lord. The blood of Jesus therefore covers me and sanctifies me" Do not take your blood confessions for granted at all. It works in diverse ways.

You also have to understand that with the confession, there is no need for any physical "elements". You only say what you believe about the blood and apply it to your present situation, negating any negatives and empowering all positives.

I know a man of God in London who has seen tremendous miracles and healings just by asking the sick to say "this belongs to me because of what Jesus has done. I therefore claim my healing or deliverance". It sounds so simple but it works. You may ask me what Jesus has done. He has shed His blood for our redemption. Hallelujah!

Psalm 107:2 - Let the redeemed of the LORD say so, whom he hath redeemed from the hand of the enemy;

As a child of God, you must continue to make this confession of redemption by the blood.

1 Cor. 1:18 - For the preaching of the cross is to them that perish foolishness; but unto us which are saved it is the power of God.

Rev. 12:11 - And they overcame him by the blood of the Lamb, and by the word of their testimony; and they loved not their lives unto the death.

Also learn to avoid negative confessions as they tend to neutralise your positive confessions and rob you of your testimonies.

Pro. 13:2 - A man shall eat good by the fruit of his mouth: but the soul of the transgressors shall eat violence.

7 Major Confessions You Need To Make With the Blood of Jesus

1. Redemption or Salvation

Salvation is always activated by confession. You cannot be saved until you confess the Lordship of Jesus Christ with your mouth (except other means has to be used for health reasons). You only become born again by your confession of faith in Christ's Lordship and atonement.

Rom. 10:9 - That if thou shalt confess with thy mouth the Lord Jesus, and shalt believe in thine heart that God hath raised him from the dead, thou shalt be saved.

Eph. 1:7 - In whom we have redemption through his blood, the forgiveness of sins, according to the riches of his grace;

1 Pet. 1:18 – 19 - Forasmuch as ye know that ye were not redeemed with corruptible things, as silver and gold, from your vain conversation received by tradition from your fathers;

19But with the precious blood of Christ, as of a lamb without blemish and without spot:

Confession Example: Lord Jesus Christ, I thank you for the blood you have shed for the redemption of all who believe. I confess that I believe in the complete work of redemption through your blood and I receive it with gratitude. Today, I confess you as my Lord eternally. Let the blood wash me clean and write my name in the book of life. Amen.

2. Cleansing

It is exceptionally needful when you feel dirty or sinful especially after committing any sin (please note that this is not an excuse to keep sinning or sin wilfully) that you get back into the light of holy living and into fellowship and make a confession.

Of course you must repent and ask for God's forgiveness but sometimes, the enemy can continue to make you feel so dirty that you feel discouraged from coming into His presence or fellowship. In such situations, confess the power of the blood to cleanse you by faith and feel cleansed.

1 John 1:7 - But if we walk in the light, as he is in the light, we have fellowship one with another, and the blood of Jesus Christ his Son cleanseth us from all sin.

Psalm 51.7 – Purge me with hyssop, and I shall be clean: wash me, and I shall be whiter than snow.

1 John 1:19 - If we confess our sins, he is faithful and just to forgive us our sins, and to cleanse us from all unrighteousness.

Confession Example: Dear Jesus, thank you for the blood that is powerful enough to wash me of all sins. I submit myself for the cleansing with your blood and I declare that I am clean through your blood. Satan, you have no right in me. I am washed in the blood of Jesus Christ. I am clean in Jesus' name. Amen.

3. Justification –

The blood of Jesus qualifies you for every great thing that God has for His children. Satan easily makes God's people feel they are not worthy of something because of something they did in the past. It doesn't matter what you did, the blood has justified you and made you as though you never sinned. Make your confession boldly.

Is. 61:10 - I will greatly rejoice in the LORD, my soul shall be joyful in my God; for he hath clothed me with the garments of salvation, he hath covered me with the robe of righteousness, as a bridegroom decketh himself with ornaments, and as a bride adornethherself with her jewels.

Rom. 5:9 - Much more then, being now justified by his blood, we shall be saved from wrath through him.

Heb. 10:14 - For by one offering he hath perfected for ever them that are sanctified.

Confession Example: I am God's precious child. I have been bought with the precious blood of Jesus. I am worthy of every blessing because the blood of Jesus has qualified me. Amen.

4. Sanctification

To be sanctified means to be made holy. The blood of Jesus has made us all holy no matter what we have done in the past. The blood also empowers us to live holy even now. By the blood you can be Holy. You can lose the appetite for sin by the blood.

1 Pet. 1:1-2 - 1Peter, an apostle of Jesus Christ, to the strangers scattered throughout Pontus, Galatia, Cappadocia, Asia, and Bithynia,
2Elect according to the foreknowledge of God the Father, through sanctification of the Spirit, unto obedience and sprinkling of the blood of Jesus Christ: Grace unto you, and peace, be multiplied.

Heb. 13:12 - Wherefore Jesus also, that he might sanctify the people with his own blood, suffered without the gate.

Confession Example: By the blood of Jesus, I have been made holy. All my past sins have been washed away in the blood. The blood also gives me the power to overcome every temptation to sin.

By the blood I can and will live a holy life the rest of my days. Thank you Jesus, for the blood that makes me holy. Amen.

5. Claiming Life

The enemy can attack your life and give you reasons why you must give up and allow him to sift you. He either would like to kill you physically or spiritually.

Your confession of faith in the blood of Jesus will always deliver you from such attacks.

Lev. 17.11 - For the life of the flesh is in the blood: and I have given it to you upon the altar to make an atonement for your souls: for it is the blood that maketh an atonement for the soul.

John 6.53-57 - Then Jesus said unto them, Verily, verily, I say unto you, Except ye eat the flesh of the Son of man, and drink his blood, ye have no life in you.

54 Whoso eateth my flesh, and drinketh my blood, hath eternal life; and I will raise him up at the last day.

55 For my flesh is meat indeed, and my blood is drink indeed.

56 He that eateth my flesh, and drinketh my blood, dwelleth in me, and I in him.

57 As the living Father hath sent me, and I live by the Father: so he that eateth me, even he shall live by me.

Confession Example: Through the blood of Jesus, I have life eternal. The blood protects me and covers me both spiritually and physically.

The enemy has no right to touch my life in any way. By the blood, I claim my right to life in Jesus name. Amen.

6. Claiming Intercession

You can always ask for the blood of Jesus to intercede for you especially in situations when you need God's mercy. There are situations when you feel you don't qualify. You can hide behind the blood and ask the blood to speak for you.

Heb. 12.22-24 But ye are come unto mount Sion, and unto the city of the living God, the heavenly Jerusalem, and to an innumerable company of angels,

23To the general assembly and church of the firstborn, which are written in heaven, and to God the Judge of all, and to the spirits of just men made perfect,

24And to Jesus the mediator of the new covenant, and to the blood of sprinkling, that speaketh better things than that of Abel.

Confession Example: Lord Jesus, I know that your blood was shed for me so that I can access things that would normally be impossible for me to access. As I go through this situation, let your blood speak better things on my behalf and help me to come through successfully. Amen.

7. Access to God's presence

Just as the High priest could not enter into the Holy of Holies without blood, so can we not enter into the presence of God without blood. Thankfully, the blood of Jesus has been shed for us, giving us the grace to enter into His presence. You know that the presence of God can also be referred to as His anointing. The blood of Jesus therefore empowers you to live an anointed life in His presence. Glory!

Heb. 3:1 - Wherefore, holy brethren, partakers of the heavenly calling, consider the Apostle and High Priest of our profession, Christ Jesus;

Heb. 10:19-22 Having therefore, brethren, boldness to enter into the holiest by the blood of Jesus,

20By a new and living way, which he hath consecrated for us, through the veil, that is to say, his flesh;

21And having an high priest over the house of God;

22Let us draw near with a true heart in full assurance of faith, having our hearts sprinkled from an evil conscience, and our bodies washed with pure water.

Confession Example: Father God, I come into your presence not in my own right but through the precious blood of Jesus. May I dwell in your presence and under your anointing all the days of my life through the blood of Jesus. Amen.

Eleven

12 VERY IMPORTANT CONFESSIONS TO MAKE WITH THE BLOOD OF JESUS

In addition to the confessional uses mentioned in the previous chapter there are other instances or situations where we can claim victory by confessing the overcoming power of The Blood of Jesus over the said situation. The following are just twelve of such situations.

1. Claiming Healing

The blood of Jesus was shed for our redemption from all things that pertain to death. Sickness is one major thing that Jesus died for. This is why He asked His disciples to heal the sick. He won't ask them to heal the sick if He wasn't willing to heal.

Throughout Jesus' ministry on earth he never denied anyone who asked for healing. He healed them all and you won't be an exception. Claim your healing through your faith confessions.

Rom. 6:23 - For the wages of sin is death; but the gift of God is eternal life through Jesus Christ our Lord.

Heb. 9:22 - And almost all things are by the law purged with blood; and without shedding of blood is no remission.

Is. 53:4-5 Surely he hath borne our griefs, and carried our sorrows: yet we did esteem him stricken, smitten of God, and afflicted.

5But he was wounded for our transgressions, he was bruised for our iniquities: the chastisement of our peace was upon him; and with his stripes we are healed.

Confession Example: Jesus has borne my sicknesses on the cross of Calvary. By His stripes I am healed. Let every sickness get out of my life for I am redeemed with the precious blood of Jesus. Amen.

2. Purging your conscience from the debilitating effects of old sins

Some old sins are hard to erase from our consciences. Satan takes advantage of this and makes you feel unworthy. He then tries to use your sense of weakness or unworthiness to attract you back into them. The blood of Jesus will however purge your conscience and give you power over any negative memories, giving you a sense of wholeness and worthiness. This will boost your confidence as a child of God and help you to stand for Him at all times.

Heb. 9:13-14 For if the blood of bulls and of goats, and the ashes of an heifer sprinkling the unclean, sanctifieth to the purifying of the flesh:

14How much more shall the blood of Christ, who through the eternal Spirit offered himself without spot to God, purge your conscience from dead works to serve the living God?

Confession Example: I wash myself and my conscience in the blood of Jesus. My past sins are gone forever. I am now the righteousness of God through the blood. Satan, get lost! I am clean in Jesus' name. Amen.

3. Redemption from the powers of wickedness

There are oppressive and wicked spirits of the devil lurking all around us. These spirits work their way into oppressing you, then they depress you and eventually take over your will, causing you to do things that you would normally not do.

As the book of James says that sin will always lead to death, when they have succeeded in making you do enough evil, they eventually destroy you. The blood of Jesus will always give you victory over all satanic manipulations and attacks. Just confess your victory through the blood.

Jer. 15:21 - And I will deliver thee out of the hand of the wicked, and I will redeem thee out of the hand of the terrible.

Hos. 13:14 - I will ransom them from the power of the grave; I will redeem them from death: O death, I will be thy plagues; O grave, I will be thy destruction: repentance shall be hid from mine eyes.

Confession Example: I take authority over every devil and over every work of the enemy against my life through the blood of Jesus and I declare them bound and their works destroyed in the name of Jesus. By the blood of Jesus, I have everlasting victory over all works of the devil in Jesus' name. Amen.

4. Claiming reconciliation to your original position before the fall – Friends with God.

Before our fathers, Adam and Eve fell, the Bible says there existed a bond of friendship between them and God. We are told that God would visit them in the cool of the day. The fall and sin alienated us from Him because God is Holy and cannot stand the presence of sin. You can also say that sin cannot stand His Presence.

The enemy has tried to use this alienation even against believers by making them feel unworthy to be in God's presence. Many believers see it more as work being in God's presence in prayer, bible reading, church attendance, general Christian and fellowship. Many also find it hard to maintain a daily Christian atmosphere around them. This is not of God. When we get saved, the friendship is restored. God therefore expect us to love to be in His presence.

Use the blood of Jesus to break every power of separation from God's presence and by the blood, get deeper into His presence. By the blood, get to enjoy God's presence the rest of your life.

Rom. 5:10 - For if, when we were enemies, we were reconciled to God by the death of his Son, much more, being reconciled, we shall be saved by his life.

Col. 1:20-22 - And, having made peace through the blood of his cross, by him to reconcile all things unto himself; by him, I say, whether they be things in earth, or things in heaven.

21 And you, that were sometime alienated and enemies in your mind by wicked works, yet now hath he reconciled.

22In the body of his flesh through death, to present you holy and unblameable and unreproveable in his sight:

Confession Example: Through the shed blood of Jesus Christ, I have been reconciled back to God. I have favour with God. I have the right to God's Presence. I am a friend of God. Nothing has the power to take me away from His Presence. I will dwell in the Presence of the Lord, all the days of my life, in Jesus' name. Amen.

5. Claiming the Anointing (Power of the Holy Ghost)

Throughout Bible history, there are instances where fire fell from Heaven to consume sacrifices that were acceptable unto God. When a sacrifice is acceptable unto God, He sends down His purifying power which purifies and thus justifies the one making the sacrifice after which He releases His power in their support. When Elijah's sacrifice became acceptable unto God in 1 Kings 18:36-40, the fire fell and enough power was released to destroy the prophets of Baal and to restore Israel back to God.

The fire fell on the day of Pentecost to signify the acceptance of Christ's blood on our behalf, restoring the glory that man lost in the Garden of Eden. This resulted in the release of enough power unto the disciples to preach the gospel in the face of persecution, raise the dead, heal the sick and perform miracles that defied all scientific theories.

You can through the blood of Jesus, also claim this power or anointing in every area of your life to enable you stand as a worthy witness to the death and resurrection of Christ. Without the power of the Holy Ghost, you cannot do much in the name of Jesus.

Acts 1:8 - But ye shall receive power, after that the Holy Ghost is come upon you: and ye shall be witnesses unto me both in Jerusalem, and in all Judaea, and in Samaria, and unto the uttermost part of the earth.

1 John 5:5 - Who is he that overcometh the world, but he that believeth that Jesus is the Son of God?

Lev. 9:23-24 And Moses and Aaron went into the tabernacle of the congregation, and came out, and blessed the people: and the glory of the LORD appeared unto all the people.

24 And there came a fire out from before the LORD, and consumed upon the altar the burnt offering and the fat: which when all the people saw, they shouted, and fell on their faces.

Confession Example: I confess in the name of Jesus, that His shed blood has cleansed me and made me acceptable before God. Let the fire of God therefore fall upon my life and burn every limitation or weakness in every area of my life (you can mention specific areas where you need the power). Let the power of God fall afresh on my life as it was on the day of Pentecost and make me a true witness of the power of God through Jesus Christ my Lord. Amen.

6. Receiving God's promises through the Blood

Blood has been used over the years as a means of receiving God's promises by His covenant children. The children of Israel for example were to activate God's promise to protect them from the angel of death which was to pass through the land of Egypt if they would apply blood on the lintels of their doors.

In Gen. 8:20-22 through Gen. 9:1-3, we read of how Noah received the same blessings that was pronounced upon Adam and Eve in the Garden of Eden before the fall through the sacrifice of blood. This was very precious blood as he only had two of every beast and sacrificing them would mean ending their lineage.

Our father Abraham also obtained God's promise for his life through his willingness to sacrifice Isaac, his only son.

Gen. 22:15-18 And the angel of the LORD called unto Abraham out of heaven the second time,

16And said, By myself have I sworn, saith the LORD, for because thou hast done this thing, and hast not withheld thy son, thine only son:

17That in blessing I will bless thee, and in multiplying I will multiply thy seed as the stars of the heaven, and as the sand which is upon the sea shore; and thy seed shall possess the gate of his enemies;

18And in thy seed shall all the nations of the earth be blessed; because thou hast obeyed my voice.

We have the same blessing through the blood of Jesus. The blood has been shed through which we can obtain every precious promise in God's word. Ask God to do in your life, the things He has promised in His word, looking upon the shed blood of Jesus.

John 14:13 - And whatsoever ye shall ask in my name, that will I do, that the Father may be glorified in the Son.

Confession Example: Heavenly father, your word says that you will do whatever I shall ask in the name of Jesus because of His precious blood. By the blood therefore I ask in the name of Jesus that your promise concerning (mention any promise you desire and have seen in the bible – health, holiness, wisdom, favour, prosperity etc) be fulfilled in my life. Through the blood of Jesus, I declare that your will and promises will all be done in my life in Jesus' mighty name. Amen.

7. Claiming grace to overcome weaknesses or easily besetting sins

Heb. 4:15 - 16 - For we have not an high priest which cannot be touched with the feeling of our infirmities; but was in all points tempted like as we are, yet without sin.

16Let us therefore come boldly unto the throne of grace, that we may obtain mercy, and find grace to help in time of need.

The Bible says that Jesus Christ was tempted in every way and yet was without sin. This means that sin had no power whatsoever upon Him. It may interest you to know that through His shed blood, we can partake in the same power that kept Him above sin. The Spirit of God that kept Christ above sin is transferred to us through His shed blood. This means that by the blood, we can also have power over every sin and weakness.

There is no reason therefore why you must continue to give excuses as to why you cannot stop a certain bad habit or sin. There is no reason why you must continue to suffer from the consequences of sin.

Claim grace through the blood and overcome every besetting sin once and for all in Jesus' name.

Rom. 8:18 - But if the Spirit of him that raised up Jesus from the dead dwell in you, he that raised up Christ from the dead shall also quicken your mortal bodies by his Spirit that dwelleth in you.

Confession Example: Heavenly father, through the blood of Jesus, I have the right to overcome every sin and habit that does not glorify you. There is no reason why my blessings should be hindered by sin. I therefore claim grace and power through the blood of Jesus to overcome this (mention what sins you are struggling with) sin (or bad habit) in Jesus' name. I claim victory and declare that this sin does not have any power over my life because of the blood of Jesus, in Jesus' name. Amen.

8. Claiming a hedge of protection over your life

There are five areas where the blood of Jesus covers in your life. The first place is your person.

This includes your spirit, mind, and body. Secondly, the blood covers your house which is the building itself. Do you realise there are different feelings in different houses? Some houses feel more peaceful than others. Some houses are more prone to demonic infestation because of the lack of the protective power of the blood of Jesus. Your house must be different because of the blood. Thirdly, the blood covers your family. This will include your spouse, children and any other persons who are under your care.

The fourth place where the blood covers you is in the area of your possessions and properties. Properties that are covered are exempt from the devastating works of the devourer and are thus free to prosper. Fifthly, the blood covers your endeavours, businesses and your influence. This ensures your businesses and ventures receive extraordinary favour which helps them to thrive and grow.

In the book of Job, all of these areas are mentioned as being protected by God because Job lived a holy life and kept sacrificing blood for the atonement of any sin which any of his children might have committed. You see, sin always allows the destroyer but the shedding of blood covers the sin and keeps us secured.

Job 1.4-5 And his sons went and feasted in their houses, everyone his day; and sent and called for their three sisters to eat and to drink with them.

5And it was so, when the days of their feasting were gone about, that Job sent and sanctified them, and rose up early in the morning, and offered burnt offerings according to the number of them all: for Job said, It may be that my sons have sinned, and cursed God in their hearts. Thus did Job continually.

Job. 1.9-10 Then Satan answered the LORD, and said, Doth Job fear God for nought?

10Hast not thou made an hedge about him, and about his house, and about all that he hath on every side? thou hast blessed the work of his hands, and his substance is increased in the land.

Thankfully, we do not need to sacrifice any other blood to cover for our sins. The ultimate blood has been shed for us. We are therefore free to claim God's protection in each of these areas and trust that God will do it. By the blood, we are holier and more righteous than Job. We therefore have the right to every blessing Job had and even more.

Confession Example: Heavenly Father, your Word says that Job had his hedge of protection kept over himself, his family, his house, his property and his business through the shedding of blood. I am grateful that the ultimate blood has been shed for me. Through the shed blood of Jesus therefore, I claim your protection over (mention what you want the protection on)... in Jesus' name. I declare that the enemy cannot touch ...... because the blood of Jesus speaks in my favour in Jesus' precious name. Amen.

9. Claiming access to things and places you normally wouldn't qualify to access

The shed blood of Jesus Christ brings a total restoration from the fallen state of man back into the divine state in which we were before the fall. Through the blood therefore, you can access many places where your natural senses and natural position may not afford you to access. You no longer go in your name nor in your fallen state but in the name of Jesus and in your original "pre-fall" state. How did Adam name all the birds of the air, the animals in the forest and the fishes in the seas including microbial organisms? He literally could access anything and anywhere he wanted to without any limitation.

I dare say that by faith and through the blood of Jesus, we can have the same unlimited access to anywhere and anything we need to access. If nothing was inaccessible to Adam before the fall, so can it be for you if you can believe.

When the blood of Jesus fell on the ground on the day of His crucifixion, the Bible says that the earth shook. The shaking of the earth released every grace that was being withheld from humanity. All strongholds gave way.

The Bible also says that darkness fell on that day in broad day light. This was to give God's children access to every secret that hides itself in the guise of light. By the blood, we can clearly see and differentiate between light and darkness no matter the time of the day or the place of the event. Every hidden truth must be revealed through the blood.

Another thing that happened on the day of the shedding of Jesus' blood was the tearing of the temple veil in two from top to bottom. The blood then qualified every believer to have access to the holy of holies. Stop belittling yourself. Stop limiting yourself by hiding behind fake humility. You are who the Word of God says you are through the shed blood of Jesus. Be bold and access every height and every depth you require in Jesus' name.

Eph. 3:12 In whom we have boldness and access with confidence by the faith of him.

Eph. 1:18-23 The eyes of your understanding being enlightened; that ye may know what is the hope of his calling, and what the riches of the glory of his inheritance in the saints,

19And what is the exceeding greatness of his power to us-ward who believe, according to the working of his mighty power,

20Which he wrought in Christ, when he raised him from the dead, and set him at his own right hand in the heavenly places,

21Far above all principality, and power, and might, and dominion, and every name that is named, not only in this world, but also in that which is to come:

22And hath put all things under his feet, and gave him to be the head over all things to the church,

23Which is his body, the fulness of him that filleth all in all.

Confession Example: I thank you my Heavenly Father that through the blood of Jesus, I can access everything and every place that need to access. I declare in the name of Jesus therefore that nothing is off limits to me because of what Jesus has done. I have access to (mention what you need access to) through the shed blood of Jesus Christ my Lord and Saviour and nothing shall be kept away from me in Jesus' name. Amen.

10. Claiming Royalty and Dominion through the blood.

Many believers live battered live in near slavery all their lives because they do not know or activate what the shed blood of Jesus represents for them. The Bible clearly says in Rev. Chapter 5 that He has redeemed us from every or any type of background and made us Kings and priests to reign. Break free therefore from the life of serfdom and take your God-given position of royalty in Jesus' name. This is not in your name or through your own achievements. It's all through the shed blood of Jesus. We receive it by faith.

Rev. 5:9-10 And they sung a new song, saying, Thou art worthy to take the book, and to open the seals thereof: for thou wast slain, and hast redeemed us to God by thy blood out of every kindred, and tongue, and people, and nation;

10 And hast made us unto our God kings and priests: and we shall reign on the earth.

Tit 2.14 - Who gave himself for us, that he might redeem us from all iniquity, and purify unto himself a peculiar people, zealous of good works.

1 Pet. 2:9-10 But ye are a chosen generation, a royal priesthood, an holy nation, a peculiar people; that ye should shew forth the praises of him who hath called you out of darkness into his marvellous light:

10Which in time past were not a people, but are now the people of God: which had not obtained mercy, but now have obtained mercy.

Confession Example: I thank you my Heavenly Father that through the shed blood of Jesus Christ, I am free to reign. I therefore declare my freedom from anything that enslaves. I break free from poverty and serfdom. I declare that I am King. I declare that I am a priest through the shed blood of Jesus. Let royalty manifest in my life from today. Let the honour of priesthood be evident in my life from today in Jesus mighty name. Amen.

11. Claiming Boldness

One major way in which the enemy succeeds in destroying God's children is in the area of boldness. We are children of faith and faith cannot work without boldness. When the enemy therefore succeeds in making us timid as children of God, he succeeds in limiting our faith, thereby rendering us powerless in all our endeavours.

The blood of Jesus has however purchased for us, a spirit of boldness which when appropriated, empowers our faith to deliver wonders.

2 Tim. 1:7 - For God hath not given us the spirit of fear; but of power, and of love, and of a sound mind.

Without boldness, our testimony will forever be limited but thank God for the Spirit which we have through the shedding of the precious blood of Jesus. You can also claim boldness and accomplish great things in the Lord.

Acts 4:29-30 And now, Lord, behold their threatenings: and grant unto thy servants, that with all boldness they may speak thy word,
30 By stretching forth thine hand to heal; and that signs and wonders may be done by the name of thy holy child Jesus.

Signs and wonders follow those who are able to manifest their faith boldly. If the apostles claimed their right to boldness in order to manifest their inheritance, you and I need to do the same.

Confession Example: Father, I thank you for the blood of Jesus which paves the way for me to receive your spirit of boldness. I declare in the name of Jesus that I do not have the spirit of fear. Through the blood of Jesus, I have the spirit of boldness. I am not afraid of anything for He that is in me is greater than anything that is in this world. I am an overcomer. I am a winner. By the blood of Jesus, I can do anything. I can accomplish great things in Jesus' mighty name. Amen.

12. Claiming Prosperity

The Bible says that God wants us to prosper so far as our souls are prospering. Our souls are set on the path to prosperity the moment we get born again. As we continue in the word, our minds are renewed so that we can think like God thinks, talk like God talks and act like God acts. This is called faith. Once faith begins to grow in us, prosperity becomes automatic but it all begins first with salvation. We must allow the blood of Jesus to wash us clean so we can prosper. Through the blood, we can have every grace to prosper.

3 John 1:2 - Beloved, I wish above all things that thou mayest prosper and be in health, even as thy soul prospereth.

Confession Example: Father, your word says I have the right to prosperity through the shed blood of Jesus Christ. I thank you for this blessing and I receive it in every area of my life. I declare that through the blood of Jesus, I cannot be poor. I reject every power of poverty from my life and declare that the rest of my life will be blessed and prosperous because of the blood of Jesus in His mighty name. Amen.

Twelve

PRAYING THE POWER OF THE BLOOD OF JESUS OVER YOUR CHURCH (AND/OR YOUR FAMILY)

In chapter four, we learnt about how the blood of Jesus plays six vital roles in His body (the body of Christ, the church) to keep it healthy and growing the same way our blood helps our physical bodies to keep healthy and growing.

I have learnt over the years that some things that are rightfully ours will still not be handed over to us until we demand them. John Wesley once said "It seems God is limited by our prayer life – that He can do nothing for humanity unless someone asks Him" The blood of Jesus is ever so powerful to work in our churches but we have to ask Him to effect the things we need of Him.

I have deliberately put these prayer points here because you have a responsibility to pray for your church. Many Christians of today are deficient in prayer and if we pray at all, it is mostly about our own needs. Please know that your prosperity is connected to the prosperity of your church. If your church enjoys peace, you will enjoy peace too. For in the peace of your church, your pastor can keep his focus on the word and prayer for your wellbeing. Where the church enjoys peace, your pastor will preach the right messages that will feed your spirit, increase your faith and bring you breakthroughs.

Psalm 23:1-2 - The LORD is my shepherd; I shall not want.

2He maketh me to lie down in green pastures: he leadeth me beside the still waters.

God can only bring you to the place where you lack nothing if your church can become the place of green pastures in the Word and still waters in the fellowship with the Holy Spirit. Fight for the peace and prosperity of your church through effective prayer.

Luke 11:23 - He that is not with me is against me: and he that gathereth not with me scattereth.

It will interest you to know that Satan will easily use you in his plan to attack the church if you do not pray for it. Praying for your church ensures that you take your place in the fight against our common enemy the devil instead of being unconsciously used by him against the church. If you don't pray for your church, you will end up gossiping and doing all manner of things that distracts the church from growth. When that happens, your own spiritual and physical prosperity will also be hindered.

Six Ways To Pray the Power of the Blood into Your Church

1. Just as blood transports nutrients into the parts of the body, the blood of Jesus draws grace and gifts from God and releases them into all parts of the body of Christ

Eph. 4:8 - Wherefore he saith, When he ascended up on high, he led captivity captive, and gave gifts unto men.

The graces and gifting of the Holy Ghost makes the church exciting and real. Christianity is a walk of the supernatural. Without the manifestations of the Holy Ghost, the church becomes just like a school or social club. Anytime a church lacks the manifestations of the Holy Ghost, it begins to die.

Your church must not die. Insist on the release of the graces and gifts of the Holy Ghost into your church by persistent prayer. You will be amazed how enjoyable your church will become when the Holy Ghost is at work.

You can get the Holy Ghost to work in your church because

Christ has already paid the price of His service through His blood. It is yours to demand and keep demanding in prayer until you have the overflow.

Prayer Example: -

Father, I pray in the name of Jesus Christ the Lord of our church, that through His shed blood, you will pour upon our church every needed spiritual nutrient in the form of the graces and gifts of the Spirit. Let the manifestations of the presence and power of the Holy Ghost become so real in our church. O Lord, release your power into our church, upon our pastors and leaders and also upon every member of our church to empower us to be spiritually healthy and grow for the advancement of your Kingdom. Stretch forth your hand and give us boldness in preaching your word and grant that signs and wonders, healings and miracles will be done in the name of Jesus Christ our Lord. Thank you in anticipation in Jesus' name. Amen.

2. **Blood eliminates waste and toxins from the system just as the blood of Jesus purges the body of Christ from sin and carnal works.**

Heb. 2:11- For both he that sanctifieth and they who are sanctified are all of one: for which cause he is not ashamed to call them brethren,

Toxins and waste are the natural by-products of going about our normal lives, eating, drinking and inhaling all sorts of foods, drinks, gases and other substances.

The same is true of believers. As we go about our normal lives in our day to day activities, we attract a lot of pollution into our spirits. These pollutions if not eliminated in time, begin to fester and pollute the entire body which is the church. It starts by polluting you and when you are polluted, you end up polluting the church.

Don't forget that you are the church. So imagine what will happen if you come with your pollution and all other members come with various forms of pollutions. The church will become spiritually sick. This is where we begin to gossip and fight and take offense about the smallest things.

Fornication and other spiritual diseases or vices creep in as well to do everything they can to kill the church.

But we thank God for the blood of Jesus. If we will get serious in effectual and regular prayer for our church and enforce the power of the blood in riding our church of all pollutions, God will hear us and our churches will continue to feel fresh and welcoming.

Prayer Example:

Father in the name of Jesus I pray that the blood which was shed on Calvary for our church will get to work now. Let the blood cleanse every member of our church from every form of spiritual pollution that seeks to destroy their lives and that of our church.

By the blood, let there be a cleansing of our church right from our pastors to the children. Let not sin or the works of the flesh have a place in the hearts of our people by the blood of Jesus. And through the blood of Jesus, let every sin that has crept in be washed away in the name of Jesus. By the blood, I declare that our church is holy. By the blood, I declare that our church is pure. By the blood, I declare that Satan has no place whatsoever in our church in Jesus' mighty name. Amen.

3. **Blood fights infections just as the blood of Jesus fights and destroys demonic contamination or activity among believers.**

Satanic and demonic activities are real. Over the years of my experience with Christian ministry, I have seen many instances of demonic activity against the children of God and the church in general. If you sit down and follow some so called westernised utopia that purports the unreality of demons, your church will be destroyed and you will be equally affected. You are the church and demons are real. Take responsibility and fight them off through the blood of Jesus.

1 John 3:8 - He that committeth sin is of the devil; for the devil sinneth from the beginning. For this purpose the Son of God was manifested, that he might destroy the works of the devil.

The blood was shed so that Satan and his cohort would be denied access and manipulation of our churches and our members. Make use of it. Many people come into our churches claiming to be spiritual who if allowed, will ruin it.

The church must constantly use the blood of Jesus to resist the activities of such people. Many in our neighbourhoods are casting spells against the church. We cannot sit down. Let us use the blood to fight them off.

Satan tries to sow discord and disloyalty among us. Let us use the blood. He often sends demons of prayerlessness, heaviness and even sexual immorality into our churches. Let us stay on guard with the blood.

Prayer Example:

Father in the name of Jesus, I pray a covering of our church with blood of Jesus. By the blood, let every plan of the enemy against our church fail. By the blood, let every work of the enemy against our church be destroyed in the name of Jesus. Let satanic Trojan horses planted within our church be exposed and destroyed. Let satanic spells spoken against our church, our pastors and members backfire by the power of the blood. Let every witchcraft activity cease by the power of the blood. I declare our church an impossible place for every devil and the death place for every satanic plot in Jesus' mighty name. Amen.

4. **Blood helps repair the body just as the blood of Jesus brings healing where there are physical, emotional or spiritual hurts in the body of Christ.**

It is normal for offences, weariness and discouragements to come as we work together as a church to advance God's Kingdom on earth. These low points however do not have to become permanent; neither do they have to have any negative effects whatsoever on the life of the church. This is because like a good manufacturer, God always has repair equipments as well as spare parts that will help us get back into action as soon as we ask of Him in prayer.

Heb. 2:14-15 - 14Forasmuch then as the children are partakers of flesh and blood, he also himself likewise took part of the same; that through death he might destroy him that had the power of death, that is, the devil;

15And deliver them who through fear of death were all their lifetime subject to bondage.

Rom. 8:28-34 And we know that all things work together for good to them that love God, to them who are the called according to his purpose.

29 For whom he did foreknow, he also did predestinate to be conformed to the image of his Son, that he might be the firstborn among many brethren.

30 Moreover whom he did predestinate, them he also called: and whom he called, them he also justified: and whom he justified, them he also glorified.

31 What shall we then say to these things? If God be for us, who can be against us?

32 He that spared not his own Son, but delivered him up for us all, how shall he not with him also freely give us all things?

33 Who shall lay any thing to the charge of God's elect? It is God that justifieth.

34 Who is he that condemneth? It is Christ that died, yea rather, that is risen again, who is even at the right hand of God, who also maketh intercession for us.

Provision has been made through the blood of Jesus as God's children to help us overcome every hitch and keep marching on. Through the blood, every situation will work for our good. God has destined us through the blood to excel. We must not allow situations to bring us down and cause us to fail. We must employ the power of the blood and cause an instant restoration so we can continue to march on to victory. We know no defeat!

Prayer Example:

Father I raise my church, pastors and leaders before you in the name of Jesus. Let every weariness, offence and discouragement be submerged in the blood of Jesus. By the blood, let there be healing where there is pain. By the blood, let there be renewed hope where there is discouragement. Let every bitterness cease. Let every distress be dissolved in the blood and let every storm cease in the name of Jesus. Let the joy of the Lord flow through our church by the power of the blood in Jesus' name. Amen.

5. It carries hormones to parts of the body just as the blood of Jesus unifies different peoples and nationalities into one people called the body of Christ.

Blood is a unifying agent. It helps by putting the whole body into a common purpose irrespective of how the other parts feel or want to behave. It is the same with the body of Christ.

In a healthy church, it is common to see people of different age brackets, different sex designations, different nationalities, and different socioeconomic and cultural backgrounds.

Only the blood of Jesus, can work to keep us in the unity of the Spirit and in the bond of peace. The blood will bring so much unity and keep your church as a single family irrespective of the natural differences.

If you want a church where no one feels left out, pray. If you want a church where there is no sexism, pray. If don't want a racist church, pray. If you want a church where no one hijacks the flow, pray (put) the blood to work.

Rev. 5:9-10 - And they sung a new song, saying, Thou art worthy to take the book, and to open the seals thereof: for thou wast slain, and hast redeemed us to God by thy blood out of every kindred, and tongue, and people, and nation;

10And hast made us unto our God kings and priests: and we shall reign on the earth.

Prayer Example:

Father I pray in the name of Jesus that your Word comes to pass in our church as it is written in Rev. 5 that you have redeemed us by your blood from every kindred, and tongue and people and nation. Let every spirit of strife and separation be cast out of our church through the power of the blood in the name of Jesus.

I cast out every spirit of racism, sexism, and social classifications in Jesus' name. I declare that by the blood, we are one family. I declare that the blood of Jesus washes away all differences and makes us one people. By the blood, we refuse every plot to set us up against each other. We are one! We are united through the power of the blood in Jesus' name. Amen.

6. **It acts as a thermostat to regulate the body temperature just as the blood of Jesus covers the natural differences and extremes among God's people and brings them to the common place called a people "Redeemed by the blood"**

Blood serves as a thermostat to regulate and maintain our body temperatures at the right levels at given times. And what would we do without the blood of Jesus given the different interpretations and understandings we have in the Word of God.

It will interest you to know that in every church, there are people who do not believe in everything that are espoused as doctrine. Some members of tithe believing churches do not believe in tithing.

Some members of tongues speaking churches do not believe in speaking in tongues. The list could go on and on. Some in the same church believe the pastor must be honoured in a special way, others believe he must be treated in the same way as all members are treated.

Some like a certain pastor or music minister more than the other. We cannot go on as one body if the blood does not intervene.

Rev. 7:9 - After this I beheld, and, lo, a great multitude, which no man could number, of all nations, and kindreds, and people, and tongues, stood before the throne, and before the Lamb, clothed with white robes, and palms in their hands;

Eph. 4:3-6 - 3 Endeavouring to keep the unity of the Spirit in the bond of peace.

4 There is one body, and one Spirit, even as ye are called in one hope of your calling;

5 One Lord, one faith, one baptism,

6 One God and Father of all, who is above all, and through all, and in you all.

Without the unifying work of the blood of Jesus, our churches will become places of arguments and litigations. Just as the blood regulates the body temperature, let the blood of Jesus regulate the temperature of your church. Pray the blood to even out individual differences and bring everyone under the subjection of the leading of the Holy Ghost. You will see a great difference in your church and great grace and peace will abound towards every member. You will be happy to belong to such a church.

Prayer Example:

Father in the name of Jesus Christ, let every selfish and personal opinion in our church be submerged in the blood of Jesus. By the blood of Jesus, I bind every spirit of dissention and rebellion at work within our church. I bind every murmuring and whispering spirit in the name of Jesus.

By the blood, let every member of our church become totally subject to the leading of the Holy Ghost. Let personal opinions die.

Let the opinion of the Holy Ghost reign in our church. I declare in the name of Jesus that there shall be no factions in our church.

There shall be no rebellion in our church. By the blood, we are of one mind! By the blood, we agree! By the blood, we are of one voice at all times in Jesus' precious name. Amen.

God bless you for standing in the gap for your church. Don't forget that the prosperity of your church is your own prosperity. Don't let it be a one off thing. Keep on praying for your church and encourage all other members to pray for their churches. God hears prayer and if we can all continue to pray, His church will surely be built, and the gates of hell shall not prevail against it. Remain blessed and may the blood of Jesus keep you and your church forever winning in Jesus' mighty name. Amen.

BECOMING BORN AGAIN

Dear Friend,

God bless you for your interest in The Blood of Jesus, It's Power and How to use it. I trust you have been blessed immensely as I was by these revelations.

Please be reminded however that the power in the blood of Jesus is, as mentioned earlier in the book, only available to those who have accepted that Jesus is God who came into the world to pay for our sins in order to reconcile us back to Himself.

You must repent from every known sin and ask Jesus to wash them away from your life. You must also be willing to trust Him and follow His lordship for the rest of your life. This means studying His teachings by reading your Bible and attending a good Bible believing church where you will be taught how to live for Christ. You must also endeavour to obey the things you are taught and also ask Him to fill you with His Holy Spirit. This is what we call being born again. Just pray this prayer with me:

"Lord Jesus, thank you for paying for my sins, I repent of every one of them. I believe that you are the Son of God. Please wash me clean with your blood and fill me with your Spirit. I will follow you the rest of my life. Please write my name in the book of life. I declare that I am born again. I am a new creature from today in Jesus' name, amen."

Congratulations, you are now born again. Find a bible believing church near you where you can be discipled into maturity in Christ.

Do not hesitate to contact me if you need further help. The Lord bless and keep you as you walk in Him.